HOMBRE

NEW AND SELECTED POEMS

Gerard Fanning

Foreword by Gerald Dawe

DEDALUS PRESS

DUBLIN, IRELAND

ACKNOWLEDGEMENTS

This book includes poems from collections previously published by Dedalus Press: *Easter Snow* (1992), *Working for the Government* (1999) and *Water & Power* (2004).

Some of the new poems, or versions of them, first appeared in the following: *A Meath Anthology, An Sionnach, Captivating Brightness* (Ballynahinch Castle Hotel/Occasional Press), *The Irish Times, London Review of Books, The Manchester Review, New Hibernia Review, Our Shared Japan, Ploughshares (USA), The Poetry Programme* (RTÉ), *Poetry International, Poetry Ireland Review, Southword, Sunday Miscellany* (RTÉ), *The Warwick Review* and *Wingspan: A Dedalus Sampler.*

'Prayers at The Coal Quay' and 'The Stone House: Dromod Harbour' were adapted by the composer, Ian Wilson for his *Harbouring* suite (2008).

The author acknowledges Bursaries from The Arts Council / An Chomhairle Ealaíon in 2006 & 2010.

Parts of Gerald Dawe's foreword were previously published in review form in *The Irsh Times.*

HOMBRE

NEW AND SELECTED POEMS

First published in 2011 by
The Dedalus Press
13 Moyclare Road
Baldoyle
Dublin 13
Ireland
www.dedaluspress.com

Editor: Pat Boran

ISBN 978 1 906614 38 6 (paperback)
ISBN 978 1 906614 39 3 (hardback)

Dedalus Press titles are represented in North America by
Syracuse University Press, Inc., 621 Skytop Road,
Suite 110, Syracuse, New York 13244,
and in the UK by
Central Books, 99 Wallis Road, London E9 5LN

Cover image © Andrew Rich / iStockphoto.com

The Dedalus Press receives financial assistance from
The Arts Council / An Chomhairle Ealaíon

for Bríd

Contents

from EASTER SNOW (1992)

from WORKING FOR THE GOVERNMENT (1999)

from WATER & POWER (2004)

NEW POEMS (2004-2010)

Foreword

S YNOTT'S WAS A WELL-KNOWN BAR on South King Street in off
Dublin's St. Stephen's Green, much frequented by
Gaeilgeoirí, actors and writers. The great Eblana bookshop
was, after all, just around the corner in Grafton Street. In 1975 I
first met Gerard Fanning in the bar and eventually we wandered
down to the bookshop. He was a civil servant; I had moved from
Belfast to Galway and we were both 'into' poetry while
maintaining a working (and in my case, college) life as well. We
were part of the David Marcus 'stable' of poets and fiction writers,
in their early twenties, proudly publishing in 'New Irish Writing'
in *The Irish Press.* Gerard had been editing the *UCD Broadsheet* as
well as being one of the editors of *St. Stephen's,* published out in
University College Dublin in Belfield. He had asked me for poems
and from that time we swapped poems in the post and wrote notes
back and forth. The business of poetry, and much else, has kept us
in touch ever since.

I have been a fan of Fanning's poetry since those first poems
started to appear in the early 1970s. A little like Padraic Fallon,
Fanning waited the best part of 20 years to see *Easter Snow* (1992),
his first collection, in print. Devoid of any easy category by which
to peg them, Fanning's poems owe more to time than they do to
particular places. Although many poems begin in definite settings
—Dublin, Clifden, Vancouver—they end up in no-man's-land,
inside somebody's head or panning across a freeze-framed city or
landscape. *Easter Snow* is about how and why such journeys are
made. Divided into 'The Conquest of Djouce' and 'Unregistered
Papers', the two complementary sections of *Easter Snow* amounted
to a bundle of questions concerning faith, contentment, desire,

failure and ambition. The figures of Fanning's poems get by in spite of their spectacular backgrounds and generally against the odds:

> In the swarm of tonight's radio
> An awkward motif
> Is *Midnight In Moscow.*

If there is a joker in this pack of poems, it is the poet's own voice, asking us in slightly Beckettian disdain and self-mockery: *Is this a safe place, or what?* Hardly, but the poems of *Easter Snow* make this place, wherever that may be, livid with definitive light and certain perceptions. As the poet remarks in 'The Belfast Train', 'Word gets through'.

Indeed, if you take a walk down towards Dún Laoghaire's famous harbour in south country Dublin, just under the refurbished fountain, a remnant of imperial Ireland, you will find engraved on a stone plinth 'Asylum Harbour', a poem commissioned by Dún Laoghaire Harbour Company. The poem by Gerard Fanning is dedicated to the workers who built the harbour and it is a perfect piece in a perfect setting. In its place of honour it is due civic recognition for a poet who has been quietly but consistently charting what he describes in 'Asylum Harbour' as the sonar and sirens of memory.

Writing a highly distinctive, unforced and resonant poetry, Fanning developed his range and pitch from *Easter Snow* to the subsequent collections, *Working for the Government* (1999) and *Water & Power* (2004). In *Canower Sound* (2003), an interim volume, he produced a long poem of (mostly) inter-related couplets, snapshots of a real west of Ireland coastline but also of powerful illuminations of the self caught in the cross-lights of changing times and other places. The relish for particular worlds of the here and now rebound against what the Internet refers to spookily as 'unknown zones':

Now that everyone is gone,
Nothing interrupts silence
Except a goat's song.

As is characteristic with Fanning's allusiveness it really doesn't matter that much if the reader picks up the reference—in this case, to Dermot Healy's novel. The visual world that has been at the heart of Fanning's work takes over in *Canower Sound* a new-found definition and there is a confident delight in seeing it revealed in the nimble images of what is effectively the bones of an 'epic' poem.

In 1974 or so the film *Chinatown* hit the streets and in that tale of the mispronounced JJ Gittes's uncovering of the deadly truths behind water and power, Fanning stored up a tone of delivery and a way with the world which would find expression many years later in *Water & Power*. A slow deeply-charged organic process of retrieval and re-imagining that seems itself to belong to a different order of making art.

It occurs to me, looking back now, that Gerry Fanning was laying down the imaginative foundations for his own imaginative country well in advance of the finished products that are gathered in *Hombre*, this wondrous collection of almost forty years of his poems. Indeed it is a bit of a shock to think of *forty* years so formally fresh and vividly present are these poems.

From the film and music of North America, to the journeys in and around familial landscapes of the northern coastline of Louth, towards the west coast of Ireland and within the streetscapes of his own south county Dublin home, Fanning's poetry is well stocked with what he loves and knows about the life he leads, the books he reads, the music he listens to, the films he sees. *Hombre* captures all this liveliness with a lithe yet steely appreciation of not only what is good, but what is best.

Hombre simply sounds like one man talking in the reasoned and matured voice of experience while in the inner chambers of

13

these crafted lines you might also make out an innocence and relish in just being here, amidst the throng; seeing things as if for the first time. There is a humane and accepting voice in these poems with which one can identify from start to finish; a sympathetic listening too for what comes back from the world; the anxious, the tragic, the lost as much as the soulscape of stillness and silence—the terrain of the intriguingly different and the new. Without strain or stress, beneath the surface of *Hombre* a worldview takes shape.

Gerald Dawe

from **Easter Snow**
(1992)

Waiting on Lemass

It is nineteen sixty-two
or -three and we are playing soccer
in fields laced with the sheen of bamboo.

In the air that turns
amber like sally rods,
somewhere out of picture

a man is hitting golf balls
as if there was no tomorrow.
He slouches towards the sycamore shade

searching for what couples
might be lying in the seed beds
or that tall grass

loosely flecked with rye.
None the wiser, we walk home
under the beige satellites

that roll in the ether of themselves,
while all about,
a blaze of radio perfume

speaks of a man
moving his ships on soup-like waters,
or a president slumped

on his girlfriend's knee,
as here our long druid leaders
wander through the closing zones,

their autistic god
commanding options in the street,
the curfew till the white hour.

Travelling Light

Before Christmas, the small gatherings
in banks and corporate offices, after hours,
mime the end-of-year parties.
I watch a brave middle-income troupe
in St. Martin-in-the-fields
rehearse the *St. Matthew Passion*,

unseasonal scores, a birth not a death,
and momentarily forgotten,
their cars, their frail insignia,
speed underground back
to the flotilla of wharfs and gardens,
where threadbare estate lines

haphazardly define that otherness
from me and these drowsy London Irish tramps
who stretch and snore in the heated pews.
When, head in hand, your face emerges,
a young woman invoking the Messiah—
blond neck bare, strings of beads

rolled between the lynx light hairs—
I relax to imbibe that phrasing
performed time and time over,
like instinct or a commandment,
and know these sometime lines are the ties
that will reluctantly, if eventually, define.

Largo

They found a body in the uplands,
a village sleeper, curled in the furred snow,
not caring to go on.

When we examine the ice-clean repose
a chill seeps through the jerkin sleeve,
the wire glasses telescope a score of winters,

and the padding of a strip of pine
becomes the blip in the earlobe
attaching to his heart's pace.

Might we also carry our saline bag
over the loughs and tarot,
a journey through the fleecy undertow,

past the crossroads post office,
where pension money and stamps
watermark to a like regret?

Or perhaps, if we peered into the hard lime
that freezes the channels in the trees,
we too could stare back admiring it all—

the world events comically coming apart,
and love, the measure of our lives,
billeted one month for every year.

Gas

A man is taking readings
of pump and pressure
as the red fanlight,
that bloom in the western sky,
comes down from all around.

The last cars map the globe
as he checks the oilcans,
the switch on *Mobilgas*,
and settles in the lee alcove
where his soft-back thriller
waits in its glove of chrome.

If he bothers to lock the outhouse
he will see how someone has scrawled
a message on the washroom mirror.

A Diamond for Her Throat

Your words today admonish, instruct and coil down the page
like the seamless undulations I once showed you
of an exhausted marsh near the sea.

Might the tide here, so long gone, wait somewhere out of view,
to raise our marriage bed and trail us through
that diminishing air, that congruence of unlikely events?

I rake the mulching leaves, assorted browns of bark and carrion,
and, while October fog descends, this quiet mild surround
anticipates frost, a wrinkling quilt waiting to be tossed.

An Evening in Booterstown

After cold days taking photographs
confirming the nearest coastline,
I look from your window
and see how the tramp fields
have turned to a wax impression
of the sea's other shores. Reclining
like a folded mirror, or growing
in detail just as these blank papers
on the tray near the alcove
swim in their blue chemicals,
they gather the last of Dublin's
refracted light. See there
emerging from the covering darkness
of lintels, bay-windows and shut
doors, another circle of light corrects
the skyline. Like any brief town
time has polished it, with
the sea-marsh and the harbour wall,
to a pale permanence.

The Final Manoeuvre

Living the middle life,
caught between lovers,
I was prepared for the holocaust

that never came.
Crossing years like days
on a schoolboy's calendar,

tracking without retreat,
I was the inexorable traveller
pursuing my wounded grail.

On thet chill November evening
in Glenmalure, I could have owned
the whole of Wicklow

but fences would have encouraged thieves.
So, turning in this cocoon
of soft noises

I stare smiling
toward the spark of the living,
their coloured flags weaving

a cosy fever, their loves
chased by clock hands
and a life's debris.

Lying in this damp chair,
a festering in the moor-swamp's side,
I draw a pulled curtain of hair

to keep the seasons in ebb-tide,
while this axle of earth
conceals me, composes my relief.

Daytrip to Vancouver Island

We drove through the spine of the island,
occasional clay crosses where pockets of lives
wait for rain and the mailman.

Reclining on the invisible grain of the world,
their lock-up doors, endless gardens,
dandle like uncharted nerve ends

and screen the uncut land which must lie
where the roads are still being planned.
In a filling station, burning *Mobil* gas

I bought a card of Mount St. Helens
hoping to send it to you,
a slight tremor to conceal

like the shy scooped up lunar dust
or the ash that basks hereabout
in a relaxed stare, on temperance houses,

Salvation Army platforms
and the batten wooden concaves
of the various sun worshippers.

The sea at Victoria was no surprise—
couples promenading, gazing at Japan,
horizons defined in snug harbour lights

all mapped, all comprehended
like the fading zones of space.
Nightfall, and we rode the ferry

back to our miniature selves
caught smiling on the mantelpiece,
delighted it could be so simple.

Elizabeth, Elizabeth, what can I tell you—
how the comforting life of car explorations,
or the Polaroid guide to the narrative,

ignores the constant filling of the water barrels
and the nocturnal gauze of happenings
as natural events for sleeping through?

Matt Kiernan

He tries to explain how a gift emerges
singing from the shadows, how holding
the reamer like a baton
conducts receding melodies,
and how rhythm runs
like a finger through a stencil in his brain.
The radio light trembles,
the battery bleeds in its cage,
and when at last he plays
the air is as true as the quiet inflection
of Easter snow settling in its drifts of blue.

Film Noir

From the window of this hotel room
I see the uptown office
sweltering as it turns away from light.

Deep in the margins of these afterhours,
in the dun conveyance of apartment houses,
words like *alimony* and *realty*

animate the couple
who have just walked in from the street.
The fan has been dismantled for repair,

and, though there is latent mischief,
this is not serious.
The man who gestures to a fault

will explain the value of nothing,
and, in the time it takes to inch the door ajar,
someone teases out the frame.

Philby in Ireland

Nightfall, and we have driven out
from the warm lights. The thick fog
circling the hill's base corrodes
our white car as it stalks the incline.

From this high air we can see
the crawling streets, trucks and buses
wheeling in their correct motions—
trails leaving a decipher of rests.

Somewhere in this parallel of workings
men catalogue the labyrinth of the city,
and deep in its crushed underbelly
we meet and copy the blueprints

of a world drawn out on long papers.
Lives collapse if we fail, for our work,
though underhand, is significant.
Like priests we are diligent or we do not

believe. Abandoning cars, we move down
to the murmuring inlets, wide lagoons
cheeping at the breaker wall. We sail out
adrift in the wider perspective.

Philby's Apostles on Merrion Strand

All of these beaches—
mist drenched in wide lagoons—
were drawn out neatly for cartographers.

Why then do men come
hauling seismometers, their tripods
straining for the lateral view?

Silently they position
to observe the wing-beat migrations
of a city's carriages.

They may as well define
the waves gasping breath
as they check for new terminals,

for here they have come
to the outer limits,
tracing the flaw in the rounded eye,

the fault in the world's Chippendale.
Watch them tune their cackling radios
of bird-song and wind-song,

staring eastward as though
a life's objective could ring less clear
down the crowded airwaves.

Meanwhile a world of talking heads
passes their door; quiet manoeuvres
belie hidden purpose.

Sailing into Leitrim Village, 1986

William Glenn guides us to Leitrim Village
through the cuttings that furrow off the map
along the drains and bleak pumping stations
where high water often floods
and a towpath battens down
its parodic table of love seats.
In this calm wet New Barbary,
in the days that submerge the year,
we join the chatter of leavings, great events,
where in an olive-stained drinking bar,
through the dark of Ireland's holy hour,
we drift into the words of marriage.

From this end slip
we could circle in our own length,
steer the blue margin of the marine file,
nuzzling red and black
on British government charts of another century.
But the echo-sounder bleats,
the bell-stove smokes alarmingly,
and, though the balm from the doldrums' stray fog
unfurls in the rivers and lakes,
we search for the perfect hide.
These years, letting the spirit subside,
have made us nonchalant with time.

The Lawn

Hoe the black clay till its spur
resembles the dust of the moon map,
let all the sandy seas mirror the pantry floor
and let the calm that follows down
play through the agonies
of the fickle pollen storms.
Might everything find its level—
field-cow wheat, dandelion and thistle,
the grain and the tassel of a sage trampoline?
Now as shooting stars descend
I correct small contour flaws,
pencil-stroke a declining magic
on the staves for the next rendition,
and dream of a pine needle perfection
where your hint might be the blueish vein,
the charcoal in the bush soul,
the resin nibbling the membrane.

The View from Errisbeg

Robert Lloyd Praeger
called it the best in Ireland.
Climbing with three children

where ice or bulldozed shale
must have wrestled with form,
I saw the thunder of the North West Passage

pouring into a pagan bowl,
and through a muslin sheen of horseflies
I gazed like Praeger

at the magnificent loneliness of the lakes.
Weeks later in a cowering Dublin,
I stand in a blue light

and watch the smoky figure
begin to emerge,
my long lost Franklin,

whose loneliness charged the incidental
into a world-weary search
for a safe passage

out of God's bleak stare.
I stack the inky photographs—
engraved miniature journeys—

and sense wild indigo
peppering my skin,
prompting a medical note

or a bruised tattoo
to rise from the cracked calamine
for all the lost galleons

moaning on their beds of brine.
Perhaps a leisured life
becomes its own fabric,

as here in braided light,
place-names fade with the ochre sun,
my folded map tucks like an alpenstock

and I drift into the lull of mid-evening,
dreaming of an astronaut
who descends through hoar frost,

his visor blank with detail,
all the thin bleached drawings
of our winter trading ships

locked in the purple ice;
and already in the *National Geographic*
the mock-up is conceived.

Within a Mile of Dublin

Waiting for the new ice age
a fifties rucksack slung in the hall,
panniers fading into survival,
and here a bureau filled with maps—
all the bright cities that spiral out
from the paving stones of parishes
to the glass of the world savannah.

See how my child-like drawings
foretold the smoky photographs
that swam through faded oxygen,
and see how I pretend to know
the swirl of the earth's weather,
the politics of dwindling satellites—
trying to imagine the lost caresses
meandering in space. So if I draw
boundaries ravenous for acreage
I still remember where the coffee-
stained villages are breathing
beneath the listless reservoirs.

from **Working for the Government**

(1999)

Alma Again

My father has travelled down for the week-end.
He tiptoes from the scullery, yearning, I suppose,
for his smoky rooms where men exhale,
talking of horses, guineas, Redbreast
or the whiff of shag tobacco in an ox-tail.

His pipe snorts like a little pot stove
as he sneaks over the sleepers to the far bedroom.
Linen flaps in the rust-embroidered air.
End of July 1951, he comes into his own,
and I almost feel I am there.

Only my mother can say this wasn't true,
though, when she closes her eyes chanting vespers,
she reveals my snow-blind tattoo.

Leaving Saint Helen's

The swarm of black-clad novices
walking past our door
in groups of three

vanished overnight.
Now as fields
fill with rape

and the perfumed garden
reverts to pasture,
the great house resembles

an impromptu barracks.
A world is being
mobilised or demobbed,

doors flung open,
moon-dazed clocks
running fast,

and, like sappers
lost in the North Wood,
we lean to the right

feeling for balance
while the earth drags
beneath our feet.

Time is moving away.
It happens like that.
People lose interest.

Printing the Legend

The train journey into Venice
pulls across the morning swamp,
through what one painter might hold
was turmoil, written into grains and pigments—
or so our host retold.

In Ford's *The Man Who Shot
Liberty Valance* there is a similar
black and white chamber
of dots and smoke
where a train parts the prairie
like a mink admiring its coat.

These are false starts, like a false dawn,
but how else could Ford
or Fellini in *Amarcord,*
begin to print the legend
except to say, the lead story
in today's *Shinbone Star*
tells of who is the toughest man
south of the Picketwire.

Lenten Offering

Though we have nothing to show
for all our talk of drizzle, colcannon,
and a glossary of moss,
on St. Patrick's day in Bologna
we unwrap our *living shamrock*
ready to wear, conceived near
the monastic settlement of Skellig Rock.

But it refuses to reveal itself,
or to set sail in its vial of tepid water;
like a mauve lily
unimpressed to be roused so soon,
its belly shows off a spray of liver spots,
confusing seepage with a tang
of cancerous vermouth. Undaunted,
I prepare the mock silver paten
and bless the little tangle
as if we were back in our bedroom,
out of time, saying mass.

About Abstraction

No more unusual are the salmon smolts,
they flee Killary, sprouting wings,
in a droning helicopter out of their element
into the weightlessness of things.

A Map of Crumlin

Optics swam as it pawed and stretched
before coming to, with tiny fists clenched.
Somehow that spirit never stayed clear
when we sent it to London for its little acid bath,
but on the green baize of Crumlin
we idly traced its smooth belly and groin.

Now in a foolish way, as it pines
for a bed of cloves, a den of mulch and carbon
we see it as a rogue sign
to stretch the fields of turpentine,
an impression of tallow in an inky duress
to tuck and pin these shipping lanes,
these freshly dug canals,
like a spinning thurible of excess.

St. Stephen's Day

After the church service
we park beside the cemetery
waiting for the drenched mourners
to pass by.

Leading us in trenchcoats,
they resemble the break-up continuity
of that civil war film,
and we, the peripheral characters

smirking in the almost out-of-shot.
Though we may genuflect
and catch the squalls
trailing their five minute lulls of blue,

we take this chance
to stand and listen
to the bleached white epiphanies
and the little offices

where space conceives infinite space
and breviary translates into missal.
So stand clear
on this St. Stephen's day

at the edge of one version of events,
where our thinning shadows
count the hours
of the pale immaculate sun,

but fail to retrieve
the picnic sites
from Kinnegad to Kilcock,
the truck stops on Route 66.

Art Pepper Remembers Paul Desmond

The way the air shifts you would think
there was no medium out there—

all notes cut from the flame of ice
will cherish the blow-by-blow I scare
into the vacuum that is already gone.

And there is no accounting for this,
what we walk and talk in
is essentially humbling and flattering,

though what it all commands
is this somnambulant line
clouding the issue with its beat and its time.

I am riding down through smoke and vapour,
trying to remember not the air itself,
but this air, this lithe composure of song—

how the disparate necklace of plucks and beats
could challenge the dissonance of wrong.

April 1963

At the end of December with the sky dark and full
Bud Powell creates the hyphen for Dexter Gordon
in *Willow Weep For Me.* Some encouraging voice
has its moonlit brocade filtered down
as the session's altimeter prints the air of Paris 1963.

I have forgotten my classroom and Glen Gould's silent holler.
You could forget everything when days are filled
with notes like these, the tempo of fahrenheit and centigrade,
the composition of oil on frieze, though it might yet snow,
and in the morning the little footprints will be
quavers surfacing through the undertow.

Silence Visible on the Lough Inagh Road

The few lodges are closed still
and the caretaker winter staff
burn the rubbish that accumulates
in some version of prior time.
Opening windows turn and turn about,
they check paint lines,
while that skitter of anti-fowling
fondles the tied-up lake boats.
Things occur, almost without cause,
or in a dust waltzing as it falls
raised pontoons rake the lazy water,
a plateau of derricks slithers on guys
of steel, while archipelagos of sound,
those cries in slipshod time,
are the stuff of intrigue,
yet to be revealed.

Laytown Races 1959

While searching for a place to land
my beloved aviator trails his voice
like a tea stain in the sky.

For he is running dry
across corrugated chalets, open fenlands
and a prairie of saline fields.

He wonders how far above the tide mark
we should stake out his course
while reeling in a line of stage fright

and, though the radio has no report of this,
I see the shy heat of the dunes,
the beach becoming crowded

and men strolling down Tiernan's Lane.
Why then should my mother say,
in thrall to the turning of the year—

he will come from the marsh road
past the links and the bawn?
For decked out in khaki

I'll soon be called to eat or swim.
The horses are held back with bunting.
A languorous tide is coming in.

from **Water & Power**

(2004)

Offering the Light

If three white on the score board
should lead to an offer
to abandon the day's endeavour,
I'll play the night watchman

who heads for the pavilion
taking for company
a last glance round silly point,
a brief sweep of boundary and bye

and one more entry
for that loose archive,
where the real map of Dublin
is about the same size as Dublin.

A Carol for Clare

whisper your name in Phibsboro
through prison yard and hospital

tiptoe through Portobello
assembling choir and canticle

pass on the grain of Rialto
where fog and snow are audible

still the hours in Pimlico
harmonise a madrigal

lie with your ghost in Marino
shepherd the final decibel

Ludwig, Ruth & I

Gathered on your verandah we drink and talk
about neighbours in a found land. You brought
Susanna Moodie's clarity, settled in Victoria's air
but never spoke of that albino shack at Cape Spear.
Its charcoal heart on your landing now
beseeches the children to come home, safe and sound.

In this street of maple quarter lots
built for the plain man in the early 1900s,
your next-door neighbour
has summoned the municipal inspector
to translate a template of roods and perches,
to admonish the laburnum when it overreaches,
so that, in another time and far from home
when we unspool the fences, language alone
might lasso the blond interior or confuse
the world we live in with the words we use.

Asylum Harbour

for the workers who built Dun Laoghaire Harbour

When I hauled myself up on our roof
    to settle a silver-speared cowl,
    your arms and my arms aligned
with Pigeon House, Baily and Kish.

    And as for that refuge, I recall
    a funicular with its mercury tilt,
ribbons of brine on a tattered hull,
    stone men singing shanty songs.

And if their wagons of Dalkey stone
are all preserved in this box of light,
    the sonar of dying ships
    the sirens in faded livery
are in every block that groans and strains
    as foghorns plead with memory.

Teepee at Bow Lake

Tepee at Bow Lake, Medicine Hat, Alberta
July 10, the man looking towards Eden
has his mind set on the spiralling cost
of his film set, soon to be called *Heaven's Gate.*

The Cancer Bureau

The nurse paints on my puffed belly
the Load Line or the Plimsol Mark.
She says it will rise and fall through salt water
and, where tidal streams
connive to build their rudimentary dreams,
she says my weight will be greater.
So much for the spindles, pulleys and shafts
conspiring to show
my maximum permitted loading
for Winter North Atlantic, Indian Summer
and Tropical Fresh Water,
for, as I tell her over and over,
I never plan to leave this world again.

The Stone House: Dromod Harbour

Boat piers are much alike.
Stepping ashore at The Stone House,
doused in the inky stream of Acres Lake

we walk a tarmacadam line
where curvature comes together
as strands of carmine

climb through migrant sprays
of laburnum and maple.
In a wait that slowly accumulates

until too long, hours refract,
and like a tiptoeing through a glass lean-to
we examine the stills of this romance—

the trays of alpines dusted over,
the hunter's shot leaving no report,
the tennis court going under—

trying to fathom that flinty allure
as somehow the wail
of the long-haul Dublin train

recalls a man who was falling,
crying out somewhere
for his coffee-stained hill,

folding his wings as if all he desired
was a polished strip
amongst petrified pines,

where the stain of silence
would be heaven sent,
and boat piers would greet the innocent.

The Railway Guard

Past the church, a brambled lane,
the remains of dairy farms,
legal notes hammered onto fence posts
and fields of assorted grasses
burning clear to the iron track.

Out of this dry clay near Gormanston,
in the needle-white of November,
men still bring their horses down
to hug the foreshore
as if what they fear in the encroaching tide
is not the tide alone.

Moon worshippers used to winter here,
and their bitumen chalets,
in vapours of creosote,
now lie chalked-pegged for the Geiger boys
so all our bruised affection
bristles in cardoons and docks.

From such marine enamel,
sandy scores of the black and the white
might tell how we recede
in the scant world
of the bled photogravure,
but Clare smiles and whispers
that here is as good as anywhere
to mimic the salmon shoals
who never betray
what gossip might thrive
in the olive orchards and seaweed barrios.

I know that fifteen summers
spent on my knees, combing through
eel grass, sea holly, sea lavender,
could never hope to appease,
but when she walks to greet
my grandfather—the railway guard—
on his Marsh Road settee,
she is whiter than all of these.

from Canower Sound

for John & Kaye

A day so full of autumn
I am listening to the rustle of dead leaves.

Again and again the morse of repairs,
bones chattering in some oratory.

For years, the same pile of blocks
strewn on the verge like unread books.

I stumble through our Boboli Gardens,
ruins, title deeds, quills.

Surrounded by the Latin names for flowers,
I wade through a pharmacy of ills and cures.

Where the ophthalmic inspector has retired,
fuchsia and iris thrive.

The dowager's house breathes onto a vacant lot—
the *Four Last Songs* with Lucia Popp.

Like a tuning fork, or just after—
I log the grey heron, our version of the crane.

I cup an ear to the drone across the inlet—
the trigonometry of stones.

Long shadows in Cashel Hotel,
de Valera, de Gaulle, a brace of tall men.

Carrying seaweed in a samovar,
Jack Elam enters Boulger's Bar.

Waves dance ashore arm in arm
like a couple of swells.

At the hour of the wolf I improvise
a singing line for Bix and Ives.

I sleep on Bergman's ivory shore,
take auburn light from his belvedere.

Another day full of autumn
sees the kitchen garden putting on new leaves.

Wide of the Mark

I know I should prefer
the busy conflagration
of reading through chain mail,

the tickertape of frightened stock
that utters from the weathervane,
something about that moment

when a star is in the east
as a slack-jawed anchorman
or a forgotten cosmonaut

omits to emphasise
that now is too late to spray,
or the premonition—call it intuition—

that this is all by the way,
even as my nurse
is coaxing a mirror

down the lining of my oesophagus,
pointing like an idiot savant
to the very heart of things.

Everything in its Place

I glance down the windy canyons
where all the metals flow
and an American Indian
shinnies up a column of steel
retrieving core samples from far below.
Settling the rods
he follows his pit-helmet's gaze
and, in a moment or so,
a beam comes floating towards him,
making so easily
it barely ruffles the undertow.
He might be one of the high-steeled Iroquois
composing a mute score
while pursuing the hint of snow
found only in his forebear's air.
I stare through double glazing,
hugging my indoor vertigo,
and he taps for sweet air
as though in baby semaphore
a silent major chord could show
that melody we all revere.

Water and Power

My father's watch
was the only thing I wore
when I dived into the Merrimack
in the summer of 1974.

An engagement present—
it seized with rust
faster than I could grapple
with the ties of trust.

I had let slip the role
that love plays
in a sketch or a rectangle,
and, though it had some way

to tease the future,
I was unaware
of such swift currents,
nor could I dare

to travel too far out
toward the wooden pins
following their line
in the racing mill.

Even if I could jump
into the same river twice,
so the watch could regain
what it was once,

how can I mourn a proof
for shock and dust
when water and power
are what needs must?

New Poems
(2004-2010)

Still Man

The sum of what I see or believe
is simply the case, or mostly true,
and if the limits of my experience
set bounds on the way the world is,
at least for me, no doubt rivers
will soldier on even as I sleep
and fail to keep vigil at their bridges.
The truth that I am wreathed in error
allows me to retreat through the fallacy
of laws in language and broach the matter
that I am here, composing the compass
of worth, while remaining the god
of my own importance, often listless,
often singing out like Chanticleer.

A Love Story

Last night we camped
on Boss Croker's acres,
tonight we cross
a river in spate,

in the miles between
a white-haired man
carries his gospel of brake-
pads and corrugated iron

like the sheets of asbestos
which we found to our cost
when we tramped
through Kippure and Ticknock.

We cough in unison,
we argue over direction
and though we had come
in search of rue des Favorites,

to take on the low down
of its honky-tonk bars,
we bear witness to unnamed
toxins, the domestique

who gestures like a friend,
as the halting ambition
that dithers and skews
and is brought to its knees

lets us gaze again
on brownfield and edgeland
with all the aplomb
of Mir's captain.

An Old Boyne Fish Barn

You should have seen the sea in those days,
wind smoke and weeping flares washing

ashore from the barrios, all those
hesitant evacuees, as tarpaulin stretched

along Beaufort's Dyke and our drift nets
sailed through the Hebrides. Shuffling in pipe

smoke, scribbling a plume of grave longing
on the bones of a wax-bright dusk,

I stood to see the ranks at the fish barn—
open mouthed, open boxed, iced on shelf

after shelf—and stayed to inhabit
what remains for the solipsistic raconteur

who believes the weight of his vision
will dissolve with his last sigh. When I drag

a heavy catch out of the evening,
old weather, braced for meteorites,

groans like a dehumidifier and burbles
the gospel of faith and love and water.

Frank

When they dismantled the spokes of the union,
slowly but surely song lines appeared in the forest
and our charts had no more call
for the watchtowers and wire curtains
or the ready army of reserve
rusting in a century-old slumber.

And, just as in deep time we are slowly
but surely drifting from the equator,
and know less of how and when
the harrier should side with the hen,
you paused so your footfalls
could lightly strum the surges in flood water,
the banks of purple loosestrife, as you knelt
to anoint the anonymous and peripheral.

Frost Moving

In the long days between the anniversaries
of Little Bighorn and Bloomsday
what passes for the sun in these parts

beats down on the living and the dead.
A Santa Clara man
checks out of Finn's Hotel

and, just as it was
one hundred years ago to the day,
he seems to know something

we don't know. Wearing a kerchief
of dried tobacco leaves
tied loose on his throat,

braided hair like a tennis player
and the white profile badge of FDR,
he says we are all being assimilated

into the one race and, however far-fetched,
our smiles are coming together.
So when I check into Finn's Hotel

I stroke my yellow hair
and the maid in love with dew on the lens
carries my bags up a winding stair.

In My Reading

If there is such a thing anymore
as a humble servant in the vineyard

this is he, a man from the coast
home on his lunch break,

working the stooped enclosure
below me as I read and revel

in the feral words of murder
on what passes for a roof garden

with a view of Pompeii,
and further below

through French doors,
you sleeping, an afternoon to dream

or pray after the heat of love making,
just as his turning broken clay

with a method learned as a boy
becomes a kind of recreation

to justify and while away
olive baskets filled with autumn

as his mother, who once
combed her hair like Myrna Loy,

watches with approval
this noise of renewal

or so it appears
in my reading.

22/09/07

I pull onto the hard shoulder
one hundred miles from anywhere,
and, if I have mislaid sleep,
tonight or tomorrow will be
one hundred years since his burbles
and sobs reached out in the chill
of a Drogheda bedroom, a lying-in.

And from a womb that was snug and serene
or tight as a drum, to this night talk,
creeping fog and traffic scum,
or the panic left in the maw
of a feline papoose—
he has me set for the surf of the day,
will o' the wisp, footloose.

Head the Ball

Next to last page
black and white
Seurat pigments
sideburned figures
emerge from a fog
that could be from
another century
and is,
while the freezing
germ of attempted sleet
vies with the balletic
abandon
of a glancing header
resembling
a polished cue ball
either or both
bereft of a full
Bobby Charlton.
The lines down
to a bullet of text,
record the fast
forward—
a scout's eye,
a franchise for
aluminium sidings,
sharp suits on
a motor lot,
or too early
fought that brave fight.

And the legend
speaks through every
blustery Saturday
when nip
meant tuck,
and heads like
imperial eggs
were sleek
as Fabergé.

Low Tide

To get to the riverbed
and then the rivermouth
we must wade through

a heat that thrives
under the living railway arch,
past a factory compound,

the half-hearted tarmac
of a starter estate
and the bails of wire mesh

rolled on a midden
for that once-in-a-generation
floodplain. We'll pass

a school of outreach mummers
and, nearer the sea,
locals with billycans

of lugworms and maggots.
And we come, mere functionaries,
to check a minor river

and its tributaries, to count
palisades as mooring posts,
and, before the estuary can fill again,

make of this counting
a file of contention,
like the life cycle

of gypsy moths,
like the stories that fade
along excavated pots.

Magazine

I don't believe a word
of her silent stare,
in a lock-up
on a ruined lot
where the bath in the corner
is caked with blood.
She may have come
from far flung Duleek
for this tired tableaux,
but in the pewter light
of a vague afternoon,
indifference freighted with script,
she is somehow reduced
from a ragged tribe,
wearing the goodbye look,
as a given text
falls into font after font.
So take finger stain,
hair and saliva,
check the breech
in the magazine,
gather swabs to assuage
some breathless profile,
and then bring vials
into the teeming street
where anonymity is comfort,
silence is its own reward
and shrift turns up
singing its mad song.

No Going Back

Although there is no going back
this one has taken for the road.
With about half his life still to go,
he gets up from the garden bench,
unleashes the halts that bind him
to his first-born son
and exits by the long back field
with pocket watch, clip and sounding line,
signatures that have gone
as some way to talk about oblivion.
He will make for the beaches of north Dublin,
the sandy fields that mark the border
with Meath, and carry on
until the sounds for Louth become insistent,
until he can flag down
something of the spirit that we leave
behind and always seek to recall,
though where this leaves me—
a moment of elation or tardy withdrawal
years hence—is anyone's guess.

Toss

Every year they come together
like the risen sap of bamboo,
cross cut canes pitch and toss,
all the families waving, in the blossom-
laden branches of the pear trees.

Hives that once sang like choirs
lie against the gable walls
of their churches and schools,
tossed in the dust of quarantine
like old tea chests, apothecaries' desks.

They are praying, you see, with their
legs and arms coated in pollen,
that these fleeting caresses can give
hope to the smocks and dresses that live
as a ripening swell in the blossom.

Preston's

Like the stout Dimple Haig
filled with old English sixpences,

shot-packed goitre for a snipe's neck,
a last bottle of Preston's

lay on the false bottom of a chest
assembled for your grand tour.

Liniment of Boyne shank,
the very digest of a salmon run,

a worm yawning in potato sap
and a maudlin whiff from tanneries

and distilleries on the Marsh Road.
But uncorked, languorous days still show

a girl with no straps to her dress dancing
in the sun and all that bustle filled

from some other source, so now you're
doubtful whether this really is Preston's.

Tate Water

If you ask how a colour might come about,
consider the enigma of water determined by sky,
and by water I don't mean pool or rain barrel
but the wide expanse of sea or lake.
As with all things, this will depend
on where and when you look
because water absorbs light, and sea water
absorbs the larger truths of late evening
greater than the timid blue of morning.
So if sunlight entering the sea is filtered
until mainly blue and then washed back
to the observer above, who could be you
dawdling on cliff or private promontory,
then, like you, a stain of light depends on impurity
just as your purplish skin for cold or bruise
like a Doppler note brightens and passes and fades.
And if pine lakes deliver a bluish tinge,
remember in that water, increasing salts or acids
can make of the scattered light a trawl from pale
yellow to darkish brown, and, when peat is washed
down, sunlight may lose itself, cannot scatter,
and the lake becomes black. I can tell you,
impasto giving weight, how to make a profession
of mute things, but remain at a loss to figure
how the weight of water can be so sinister.

Thompson & Thompson

The stenographer's touch-typing
has me in thrall. The case

is the case in point
but her Remington is all.

She pouts, she doesn't drop
a stitch and I am aghast

to realise, so late in the day,
that the Thompson

who gave her the low-down
on shorthand and what's written

on the body, was the Thompson
who tapped out bullet points

for his other Remington—
the Chicago typewriter.

That Note

Like Miles Davis' dark Arkansas roads
the tone I was after lay listless and dreaming
as we rode the sea lanes deep in Dublin Sound.
On either side of the waters we were crossing
lay cable, freight line, pipes of city joy,
and barely visible, though gleaming and new,
an audible pitch of beads and corded wire—
weird acoustics slumbering in their alloy.

And I knew it was there, like the shudder
in a mass light-years away shows
the hidden path of a polished ball of ice
come this way with its heart on fire.
And then that solder, that rich conspiracy of brass
and copper, a flame in the blood unlike
the one-art melancholy of a cedar grove
or the straight-on certainty of a 30s autobahn,
so it feels like time itself, or a bolt
from its legions, has come to this span we inhabit,
to count on and improvise, that note.

White Page

Though the hospital nearby failed to register a temperature,
a moon rose and was full. Records show

ruffed up ranks of commonage and from asylum lots,
iris, lilac and ivy-covered trees. But these yellow fields,

with their memory of olive and cypress, tell nothing
of why he came, or why he placed an easel as dusk was setting,

nor can I gauge the hundreds of trivial impulses
coming together in their species of colour.

And through all the snows and all the winters, chalk lines list
so the very subject is lost in the accretion of tots and thimbles-full

of white spirit, just as the music stitched in the braid of a river
is enough to tip an idea of order back to the still white page.

The Verandah

Though the verandah was covered
in a patina of end-of-season hues
its primary colours were more in the way
of notional tints—sand, blown gravel,
sea salt—and there is more to this
than you might think, the scorched memory
carries on the wind to this day, as I stand
in the middle of a narrow road.

What's left is a shrinking cabin,
like Winslow Homer's *The Dinner Horn;*
got up to sing perpetual summer
as now in league with bindweed and ivy
and a young woman calling 'time',
I begin to embrace the scattered look,
cap set to the promises of others,
and then that shift while attention
runs out on a serrated scroll
at the edge of someone else's life.

The Silent Brother

Here I am, come closer,
a diminutive figure

etched in straw,
nursing the trivial

comings and goings
that will never amount

to anything.
And if company bids welcome

and the spirit withdraws,
what shrinks away

is that riddle of diminishing light,
intrigue from back yards

and honeyed winter heat,
a fleece within fleece

for the sake of a circus of sparks.
But what I do know:

like a seed stitched
in a Dutch merchant's wallet

awaiting its bead of dye,
all music lies adjacent to music

and I can live for days
in the spell of a Kyrie Eleison.

My handkerchief is blood-
flecked, I throw my whistle

to the crowd,
I am down to one key.

Variation on Blue Note

If a gourd adrift on a water meadow
levels the draught in an ocean liner,
the babbling shelves of bottled spring,
the sodden taste of smalt and beryl
should feed canals on our sister planets
and somehow yield a love supreme.

But pipes leak gas, roofs leak rain,
my blindfold phrases are tired and sprung
and dribbling back to their various parts,
the many slips that sink a ship,
port-wine stain, mizzling tributaries of vein,
feed the drip on the lip of my saxophone.
You may ache for a theme. I do not.
I love the self-fulfilling water butt.

Waking Tom

Just as in life, watching in his house,
we have agreed to disagree,
then he hums from the Irish,
'I am asleep, do not wake me'.

Weekend Away

Running a lexicon of cold and thaw
our hotel whinnies in its vatic store.

If you croon your stolen music,
I'll hum the cantata from a Japanese opera

and like shy samurai
we'll leave this world with a cosy virus

clutching a jar of wild honey
to nourish our sleep in the ocean.

But if we should drown in our own fluid
and our almanac of phrases

unravel the signature of influenza—
let that helix of clefs and quavers,

embalmer's script in Indian ink,
compose our spirited gavotte.

What Maureen Knew

Like the pitch of a Stradivarius, a lush tone cannot rely
for explanation alone on varnish or tanning,

and if I'm confusing how we come together with the vagaries
and chance of local weather, and if she appeared to prefer

the elegant sun of the bleached Alpine, in what locals call
'the forest of violins', then like something raised free range

she could emit such charcoal and honey, sufficient in voice
to remain, as her company dwindled to a few feeble out-riders

weighted with ribbon and nickel. Her winters were long
and severe, her summers cold and wet, she fed

on teeming shellfish, ice-skated near Islandbridge,
lit braziers on the frozen Liffey mouth

and found in the sally banks a world that could resonate
in the off-beat of a high-hat. And whomsoever she took

in her arms, she would chase down the lines that loll
on the coasters of an ironic equation, and leave no trace.

But the day she clutched a sweepstake ticket in a legal office
in Nassau Street in 1931, offering the camera a smile as false

as her future, was the first to hit home like a residual flower—
we should not all make of our lives a scented bower.

Who Speaks

Like the Mexican boy on his appaloosa
when asked of the 'run-off',
or 'when it happens', silent in Spanish and English,
nods to affirm—mostly at night, at different
places, different amounts each time.

Or my leaving a building through plate glass
just before the company says
their logo may as well be parallel strips of Velcro
for all the effort to find the correct door
with my purse strings and amphetamines.

Newfoundland Time

Round the planting of the Gort oak
the true magnetic poles began a variation.
Ignoring the jolt of our millennium
they reclined briefly in the Pacific Ocean
down near the island of Guam.
But when they cradled the spine of Siberia
they passed all understanding, only to emerge later
in the belly of King William Sound.

On my aimless navigations of the midland
and western bypasses, sleek asphalt
like black streams amongst saplings,
I can gain the half-hour of daylight
like the half-hour I mislaid
when I once crossed from Nova Scotia
into the bosom of Newfoundland.
So when I recite the litany of true verticals
I can realign and slip through the fissure
that folds back, not at the open field
nor at the forest, but at the border between.

NOTES

'An Old Boyne Fish Barn': p. 74. *You should have seen the sea in those days* (from Louis Malle's *Atlantic City*).

'Preston's': p. 87. The last whiskey distillery in Drogheda.

'That Note': p. 90. Written for the Sea Stallion Project.

Lightning Source UK Ltd.
Milton Keynes UK
05 April 2011

170389UK00001B/126/P